PERGAMON INSTITUTE OF ENGLISH (OXFORD)

Materials for Language Practice

CLOZE IN CLASS

Exercises in developing reading comprehension skills

WORKBOOK

Other Titles in this Series Include:

BERMAN, Michael

Playing with Words

Playing and Working with Words

Read and Recall: passages for advanced reading comprehension in English.

Take Note: materials for aural comprehension and note-taking in English.

CLARK, Robert and Jo McDonough

Imaginary Crimes: materials for simulation and role-playing.

DUNLOP, Ian and Heinrich Schrand

In and About English: authentic texts for developing reading and communication.

Matters of Moment: materials for reading comprehension and discussion in English.

HAYCRAFT, Brita and W. R. Lee

It Depends How You Say It: dialogues in everyday social English

MADDOCK, Vivienne and W. R. Lee

Getting Through: *Trinity College English*

MURRAY, Heather and M. J. Niethammer-Stott

Murder Comes to Breakfast: a detective story for intermediate students of English.

PONSONBY, Mimi

How Now, Brown Cow? A course in the pronunciation of English

ROMIJN, Elizabeth and Contee Seely

Live Action English* Series of commands for real communication

ZINKIN, Taya

Write Right: a guide to effective communication in English.

*American text with British English glosses

CLOZE IN CLASS

Exercises in developing reading comprehension skills

WORKBOOK

Alan Moller

and

Valerie Whiteson

PERGAMON PRESS

OXFORD · NEW YORK · TORONTO · SYDNEY · PARIS · FRANKFURT

U.K.	Pergamon Press Ltd., Headington Hill Hall, Oxford OX3 0BW, England
U.S.A.	Pergamon Press Inc., Maxwell House, Fairview Park, Elmsford, New York 10523, U.S.A.
CANADA	Pergamon Press Canada Ltd., Suite 104, 150 Consumers Rd., Willowdale, Ontario M2J 1P9, Canada
AUSTRALIA	Pergamon Press (Aust.) Pty. Ltd., P.O. Box 544, Potts Point, N.S.W. 2011, Australia
FRANCE	Pergamon Press SARL, 24 rue des Ecoles, 75240 Paris, Cedex 05, France
FEDERAL REPUBLIC OF GERMANY	Pergamon Press GmbH, 6242 Kronberg-Taunus, Hammerweg 6, Federal Republic of Germany

First edition 1981

British Library Cataloguing in Publication Data

Moller, Alan
Cloze in class. - (Pergamon Institute of English (Oxford) materials for language practice)
Workbook
1. English language - Study and teaching - Foreign students
2. Cloze procedure
I. Title   II. Whiteson, Valerie
428.028'8   PE1128.A2
ISBN 0-08-025350-4

Library of Congress Catalog Card no: 81-81256

Printed in Great Britain by A. Wheaton & Co. Ltd., Exeter

ACKNOWLEDGEMENTS

For permission to reprint copyright material the following acknowledgements are made:

When no-one is looking, Jerome Weidman
This is the Army, US Army advertisement
Sissy Spacek, Eve and Margaret Ronan, Scholastic Scope, © 1980 Scholastic Inc.
The books that changed my life, Scholastic Voice, © 1980 Scholastic Inc.
Jokes, Scholastic Scope, © 1980 Scholastic Inc.
Hot stuff, Margaret Ronan, Scholastic Voice, © 1979 Scholastic Inc.
Happiness is ... a Caribbean cruise, Commodore Cruise Line Ltd.
Don't blame the lions, Newsweek
How to take care of your car, Cosmopolitan
The plasterer's mate, The £10,000 a year plasterer, Bryan Waller,
    BBC Modern English MEP Ltd.
Jenny Lee at University, University of Cambridge Local Examinations Syndicate
London Transport's round London sightseeing tour, London Transport
Postcodes, Haslemere Herald
The last man to fight Ali?, Dudley Doust, The Sunday Times
A recipe for steak and kidney pie, Louis Davies, Easy Cooking for Three or More,
    Penguin Books Ltd.
Disneyland, Literary Cavalcade, © 1980 Scholastic Inc.
How to use your washing machine, White Westinghouse Corporation
A whale of a problem, The Observer Colour Magazine
When a volcano blows its top, The Observer Colour Magazine
Positive discrimination, Lisbeth Lumby, Forum, Council of Europe
Appliance guarantee, White Westinghouse
Child custody, Editorial (Mother's day in court), © 1980 New York Times
Ronald Reagan accepts nomination, Chicago Tribune
The New Zealand home in the 80's, Austin Mitchell, The Half Gallon
    Quarter Acre Pavlova Paradise

Illustrations by Rowan Barnes-Murphy

CONTENTS

INTRODUCTION

The aim of *Cloze in Class* is to develop the reading comprehension skills of intermediate to advanced-level learners of English as a second or foreign language.

The workbook contains thirty passages in which words have been deleted (Cloze procedure). The deleted words comprise grammatical and lexical items which often cause difficulties for non-native speakers of English. The student has to decide which words best fill the gaps and write them in to complete the passage.

The passages have been chosen from a wide range of newspaper and magazine articles, advertisements, brochures and letters which were originally published in Britain, the USA and New Zealand and for the most part are reproduced in their original form. They were chosen because of their interest to young adults and are graded according to difficulty.

Follow-up discussion composition and language exercises are suggested in an accompanying teachers' booklet, which also contains a key to the answers.

1. How to Steal a Car in 50 Seconds

A criminal wearing a mask gave a demonstration in Washington recently. He showed a group of US Senators how to steal a car. The man, who was introduced as Tom Brown, is serving a five-year prison sentence for car theft. This is what he told the Senators:

"I have been stealing cars for many years. In fact, I've 1_____ over 700 American-made cars. At the time of my conviction I 2_____ steal any American-made car in less 3_____ 90 seconds, and could steal most in 45 to 50 seconds.

"4_____ a bit more difficult to steal 5_____ cars. I have stolen Porsches, Volkswagens, and two Mercedes-Benz cars. The 6_____ it took for 7_____ foreign car was about three minutes.

" 8_____ you know that over a million cars 9_____ stolen in the US last year? People used to blame the 10_____ on teenagers 11_____ took the cars for a joy-ride. As a matter of 12_____ most of the cars are stolen by professionals. Yes, 13_____ has become a four billion dollar-a-year business. The 14_____ aren't sold as such. Within hours after the theft, the car 15_____ gone. It's chopped into parts 16_____ are sent to repair shops all over the 17_____. We remove the identification numbers from the parts and they are sold to legitimate garages 18_____ cut-rate prices.

"For thieves it's a very 19_____ business. I've made hundreds of thousands of dollars a 20_____. Now I'm going to show you how to steal a car. 21_____ at my tools—they're all home-made. Now 22_____ may take a little longer than usual. You see, 23_____ been in prison for a 24_____ and I'm a bit out 25_____ prac-tice."

2. A Letter to the Family

55 Shakespeare Road,
Greenside.
Sunday, March 5, 1980

My dear children,

It's hard to believe that I've been here for a month. The time passes so quickly and there's so much to do.

I've managed to see all the members of the family. I [1]_____ as much time as I can with the children. Last week I [2]_____ Mark and Michelle to the circus. ³_____ never been before as they live quite far from the nearest city and their parents ⁴_____ have time to drive them there. I ⁵_____ that's what grandmothers are for.

At any ⁶_____ Susan lent me her car—it's a brand- ⁷_____, bright red Mini. We left early in the morning so as to make a day of ⁸_____. In the morning we ⁹_____ to the zoo and in the afternoon to the circus.

As ¹⁰_____ can imagine, the children were very excited. They loved everything. Mark ¹¹_____ the wild animals the most exciting and Michelle is ¹²_____ to be an acrobat when she grows ¹³_____.

After we'd been there for about two hours we ¹⁴_____ an announce-ment over the loudspeaker. The owner of the red Mini, number PUR 727V, ¹⁵_____ requested to come to the manager's office ¹⁶_____. Naturally, I didn't know the number of ¹⁷_____ car so I left the children and went to the manager's office to ¹⁸_____ out if it was our car.

The manager looked very upset and ¹⁹_____. No one else had answered his call so I assumed correctly that it was Susan's car. ²⁰_____ that I'd left the lights on, or parked in ²¹_____ way, I wasn't ²²_____ concerned, but I didn't know why the manager looked so disturbed. He began to ²³_____ what happened and it took me some time to understand ²⁴_____ confused explanation.

²⁵_____ appears that the elephants are trained to sit on red boxes. One of the elephants ²⁶_____ escaped and when he saw the ²⁷_____ red car he promptly sat on ²⁸_____! As you can im-agine the car looked a mess. One side was squashed ²⁹_____ but it was still possible to drive. The manager assured ³⁰_____ that the circus would pay for the ³¹_____. He couldn't have been more apologetic.

The children were very ³²_____ and giggled about the incident all the way home. ³³_____ before we got there, we ³⁴_____ the scene of a serious accident. About a mile ³⁵_____ on a policeman stopped us and asked if we'd ³⁶_____ involved in the accident. I wish I had a ³⁷_____ of his face when I told him what had happened ³⁸_____ the car. I think he wanted to arrest me for drunken driving! Fortunately the ³⁹_____ were there to back me up.

⁴⁰_____ are you managing without me? Please don't ⁴¹_____ to water my plants. I'm planning to leave here ⁴²_____ the end of the month.

My love to you all,

Mom

3. When No-one is Looking

"The measure of a man's real character is what he would do if he knew he would never be found out." Thomas Macaulay

Some thirty years ago, in a public school on New York's Lower East side, a Mrs. Nanette O'Neill gave an arithmetic test to her third-grade class. When the papers were marked she discovered that twelve boys had written the same answer to an arithmetic problem.

There is ¹_____ really new about cheating in exams. Perhaps that was why Mrs. O'Neill didn't even ²_____ anything about it. ³_____ only asked the twelve boys to remain after class.

They ⁴_____ with fear in their hearts, for they knew why Mrs. O'Neill wanted to see them. They were ⁵_____ but only in part.

Mrs. O'Neill asked no ⁶_____. She said nothing. She gave out no punishment.

⁷_____ she was alone with the ⁸_____ pupils, Mrs. O'Neill wrote on the blackboard the above twenty ⁹_____ words, together with the name of the great man who composed ¹⁰_____. She then ordered them to ¹¹_____ these words into their copy-books one hundred times.

¹²_____ don't know about the other eleven boys. Speaking for ¹³_____ I can say: it was the most important single ¹⁴_____ of my life.

My life happens to have ¹⁵_____ lived up to now in a ¹⁶_____ of uncertainty, danger, and fear. It is good, of ¹⁷_____, to learn from history that all times have been full of fear,

5

uncertainty and ^{18}——————— but a man wants more than
^{19}——————, he wants tools to work with, signposts to guide
^{20}——————, yardsticks to measure by.

Thirty years after being introduced to Macaulay's words, they ^{21}——————
seem to me one of the best yardsticks I have ^{22}—————— met.
^{23}—————— because they give us a way to measure others, but
^{24}—————— they give us a way to measure ^{25}——————.

Few of us are asked to ^{26}—————— great decisions about nations going to
war ^{27}—————— armies going to battle. But all of us are called
^{28}—————— daily to make a great many personal decisions.
^{29}—————— the purse, found in the ^{30}——————, be put into a
pocket or turned over to the ^{31}——————? Should the extra change received
at the grocer's be forgotten or returned?

^{32}—————— will know. Nobody ^{33}—————— you. But you have to
live with yourself, and it is always better to live with someone you
^{34}—————— because respect develops confidence, and ^{35}—————— is
a great weapon, especially in times of fear, ^{36}——————, and danger.

4. This is the Army

TODAY'S ARMY CAN MAKE A SON OR DAUGHTER READY FOR TOMORROW.

The Army may not be the first thing you think about when you're considering your son's or daughter's future. But it's something you and many other parents should seriously consider. Because if you ¹_____ the world's changed a lot since you were 18, ²_____ should see the Army.

VALUABLE SKILLS

Today's Army is a modern ³_____. A technical Army. And it needs many sophisticated, technical skills. So we ⁴_____ young people these skills. And pay them ⁵_____ they learn.

EDUCATION

Besides being an education, the Army can ⁶_____ pay for one. We'll pay up to 75% of the tuition ⁷_____ approved courses soldiers take ⁸_____ off-duty hours. And now there are new veterans' educational benefits that can help ⁹_____ ¹⁰_____ or daughter accumulate as much as $14,100 for college in four years.

TRAVEL

Nothing helps a young ¹¹_____ view of the world better than seeing some of ¹²_____. In the Army, your son or daughter might get to ¹³_____ Europe, Alaska, Hawaii, Korea, Panama, or almost ¹⁴_____ in the continental United States.

PAY & BENEFITS

Starting ¹⁵_____ has never been higher. $448.80 a ¹⁶_____, before deductions. There are enlistment bonuses available up to $3000.

17_____ earn 30 days vacation a year. And, of course,
18_____ room, board, medical and dental care.

PEOPLE

There's no military hardware to replace 19_____ human heart, no computer to out-think the mind. 20_____ need people. We are people. We 21_____ your son or daughter to share the pride that comes from serving 22_____ country. Have 23_____ contact your local Army Recruiter, listed in the Yellow Pages 24_____ "Recruiting".

5. Sissy Spacek

What do country music star Loretta Lynn and movie star Sissy Spacek have in common? They are both connected with a movie called *Coal Miner's Daughter.* *Coal Miner's Daughter* is based on a ¹_____ Loretta wrote about her life. Sissy plays ²_____ in the movie.

"The way ³_____ got the part was kind of spooky," Sissy said. "Loretta picked me for the ⁴_____. Nobody got around to telling me, though. I was ⁵_____ *Coal Miner's Daughter* one day. I thought, ⁶_____ really like to know Loretta Lynn! Then suddenly I ⁷_____ Rona Barett on TV. She said I was going to play Loretta Lynn!

"People ⁸_____ asked why Loretta didn't play the part ⁹_____. She said, 'Look, I lived it once. ¹⁰_____ was enough!' "

To prepare for the role, Sissy traveled with Loretta ¹¹_____ a concert tour. They shared motel rooms, and Loretta ¹²_____ Sissy about herself.

"Listening to ¹³_____," Sissy said, "I picked up the rhythm of the way she ¹⁴_____. I also had to learn all of her songs and practice ¹⁵_____ her band. It made me understand how ¹⁶_____ she works."

Sissy sings in the movie, and she sounds ¹⁷_____ Loretta. She worked for months to ¹⁸_____ like that. She has always dreamed of singing on screen, though.

Sissy was ¹⁹_____ in Quitman, Texas. When she was 13 years old, she ²⁰_____ up all her money. She ²¹_____ it on a mail-order guitar.

She taught herself to play the ²²_____ from an instruction book. Soon she was playing at school assemblies. She ²³_____ gave guitar lessons—at 50 cents an hour.

²⁴_____ she was 18 years old, Sissy ²⁵_____ to New York to become a rock ²⁶_____. She hung around music studios. Her agent booked her on *The Tonight Show* a ²⁷_____ of times. But she became so nervous, she ²⁸_____ go on the show.

"29_____ a while, I knew my music career wasn't going anywhere," she said. "A friend 30_____ I try for a 31_____ called *Prime Cut.* I did. Surprise! I got the part!"

32_____ then, Sissy has starred in such movies as *Badlands* and *Carrie.* 33_____ TV, she has been in *The Migrants* and *Katherine.*

34_____ has a special way of getting 35_____ for a part. "I don't eat," she said. "I wear white. I meditate until 36_____ like a blank page. Then I become 37_____ the part says I have to be."

38_____ did Sissy get her first name? "I was 39_____ Mary Elizabeth when I was born," she said. "40_____ my brothers said it was too much of a name for me. They renamed me Sissy, and 41_____ has ever 42_____ me anything else since. Mary Elizabeth? Who's she?"

6. The Books that Changed My Life

Robin Brancato and Susan Hinton are two American authors who write for young people. They were interviewed by Voice, a magazine for young adults in the USA. Here are two extracts from the interviews.

Robin Brancato

When I was a teenager, I read a ¹_____!
That was partly because we ²_____ to a new town at the ³_____ of my freshman year in high school, and I had no old friends around. ⁴_____ I turned to books.
I liked all kinds, but ⁵_____ as now I preferred realistic fiction ⁶_____ fantasy and non-fiction. Steinbeck's *Grapes of Wrath,* Margaret Mitchell's *Gone With* ⁷_____ *Wind,* Richard Wright's *Native Son,* and Daphne du Maurier's *Rebecca* were my ⁸_____. Today, when I recommend these titles to my students, I usually ⁹_____ that they fall for them as hard as I ¹⁰_____.
Another type of writing ¹¹_____ always loved is humor. Styles change, but my favorite, James Thurber, holds up ¹²_____. I recall especially "The Secret Life of Walter Mitty" (¹³_____ is a Snoopy type, forever imagining ¹⁴_____ as a hero) and *The Thirteen Clocks,* a fairy tale. For me, the ¹⁵_____ of books is almost as important as the company ¹⁶_____ people. A good book, like a ¹⁷_____ companion, should delight you, challenge you to think, and inspire you to be a better ¹⁸_____.

S. E. Hinton

I loved *Gone With the* ¹⁹_____, *Lone Cowboy* and *Catcher in the Rye* ²⁰_____ *The Haunting of Hill House,* ²¹_____ for a different reason. I loved the epic scope of *Gone With the Wind,* admired Will James' freedom ²²_____ a lone cowboy, identified ²³_____ Holden Caulfield's conflicts, and slammed *Hill House* shut right in the middle, ²⁴_____ terrified to go on!

Of course they changed my thinking—by 25_____ me think. They
26_____ my life by improving my writing. I was already writing as a
teenager—in 27_____, I began as a child. 28_____ showed
me what could be done and how to do it.

Books 29_____ everything to me as a teenager. 30_____ have
been friends and family, escape, travel, romance, and 31_____ times a
lifeline to grab onto. I 32_____ imagine a world without books. I know
I wouldn't be able to live in 33_____.

7. Jokes

You can't take it with you

The greedy relatives were gathered to listen to the reading of the will. When everyone was seated, the lawyer spoke.

"You'll be out of here in no ¹_____," she said. "The will is only one sentence long. ²_____ says, 'Being of sound mind and body, I ³_____ every penny I had.' "

What problem?

Patient: Doctor, I ⁴_____ this terrible problem with my memory. I can't seem to ⁵_____ anything. Doctor: How ⁶_____ has this been going on? Patient: How long has what been ⁷_____ on?

Dramatic excuse

Steve went out with his friends one night. His ⁸_____ wanted him home by midnight. But he didn't ⁹_____ much attention to the time. First they ¹⁰_____ to a movie. Then they went bowling. ¹¹_____ they went to a diner for a snack. By the time they were ready to go ¹²_____, it was 2:00 in the ¹³_____.

Steve was worried about facing ¹⁴_____ parents two hours late. Then he had an idea. He ¹⁵_____ them before he left the diner.

"Hi, Dad," he said. "This is ¹⁶_____. Don't pay the ransom money. ¹⁷_____ let me go, and I'm on my way home."

The beat goes on

Angry Neighbor: I ¹⁸_____ in the apartment above you. ¹⁹_____ you hear me pounding on your ceiling in the middle of the ²⁰_____?

Fred: Yes, but don't apologize. I was ²¹_____ anyway, practicing on my trumpet.

8. Hot Stuff

A movie like this makes it fun to watch our tax dollars at work. *Hot Stuff* is a comedy based on a real-life U.S. government caper.

A few years ¹_____, our government put up funds so that undercover cops in several cities could ²_____ over pawnshops. Thieves brought ³_____ goods to them to sell. Posing as "fences," the cops ⁴_____ get the goods on burglary rings and individual crooks. The plan ⁵_____. A lot of stolen property was recovered. And a lot of ⁶_____ went to jail.

⁷_____ are the facts, fans. Now for this slightly fictionalized ⁸_____ version of them: A Miami, FL, burglary task force is about to lose those federal funds ⁹_____ its arrests ¹⁰_____ result in many convictions. In a desperate try for hard evidence on thieves, the cops take ¹¹_____ a pawnshop and pose as fences. They ¹²_____ police department money to ¹³_____ stolen goods, and hidden cameras to photograph the thieves. Business is ¹⁴_____ brisk that local mobsters try to muscle in. The cops find ¹⁵_____ up against wall-to-wall danger. The situation is serious, but the movie ¹⁶_____. How ¹⁷_____ it be, when the masquerading cops are played by Dom De Juise, Suzanne Pleshette, Jerry Reed, and Luis Avalos? ¹⁸_____ make *Hot Stuff* ¹⁹_____ of the year's coolest comedies.

9. Happiness is . . . a Caribbean Cruise

It's Saturday afternoon and you are in the cruise capital of the world—Miami—and you thought the day would never come!

1_____ feel the excitement as you enter the new port area and 2_____ the laughter of fellow passengers and begin to experience the happy feeling of the long awaited 3_____.

You're quickly checked 4_____, your dining seating is already pre-arranged, and your luggage on 5_____ way to your cabin. It seems like you just got here and yet you 6_____ already aboard and ready to sail. If your friends 7_____ see you 8_____!

And there you are on deck happily waving 9_____ as your ship slowly leaves the pier and gains momentum toward the Caribbean cruise 10_____ always dreamed of taking.

You look around as the Miami skyline disappears and 11_____ your fellow passengers 12_____ by. They're of all ages, yet they all share the same exciting anticipation of a 13_____ cruise.

14_____ is smiling, both passengers and crew, and before you know it you are 15_____ friends for a lifetime.

16_____ with whom you'll share your vacation, your shipboard life and the pleasure of your time 17_____ in the friendly Caribbean 18_____.

10. Don't Blame the Lions

The first account of Joy Adamson's death sounded all too neatly ironic: Africa's most famous animal-lover had been killed by a rampaging lion. "That's the way the world wanted to see her go out—at the claws of the thing she loved 1_____," neighbor Roy Wallace said last week. 2_____ Kenyan police commissioner Ben Gethi suspected foul play, and an autopsy confirmed 3_____ doubts. It appeared that the author of *Born Free* 4_____ been killed 5_____ a human—perhaps with a twin-edged African sword.

Wallace, 6_____ saw Adamson's body the night of her death, was struck by the lack of blood. 7_____ the autopsy, a police spokesman in Nairobi 8_____ the fatal puncture wounds on Adamson's arm and rib cage had been 9_____ by "a sharp instrument." Kenyan 10_____ settled on bad blood between Adamson and her staff as the likeliest motive 11_____ murder. "She was a talented, artistic 12_____ with impeccable standards," said a former secretary, Kathy Porter. "13_____ was always sacking the help."

Police questioned, and later 14_____ Adamson's driver, tracker and cook. They began to trace 15_____ former employees, and they also considered the possibility that the conservationist 16_____ have been 17_____ by local hunters or poachers, whose livelihood was threatened by her efforts 18_____ protect Kenya's wildlife. Meanwhile, after a small funeral, Joy Adamson's ashes 19_____ scattered, as she had wished, over the rolling plains, 20_____ she and her husband, George, raised 21_____ orphan lion cub Elsa in the 1950's and 22_____ the "Born Free" legend began.

18

11. How to Take Care of Your Car

What to do if your car won't start. The fault may be in the fuel system (the parts that feed petrol from tank to engine).

1. The system's flooded because too much fuel is circulating. What to 1_____: push the accelerator hard down and keep it there, with absolutely no pumping, as you 2_____ the ignition 3_____. Ease the pedal pressure as the engine starts.

2. The fuel lines are blocked. Tapping hard 4_____ dislodge the block.

3. You're out of 5_____.

If your starting trouble isn't in the fuel system, the ignition 6_____ which turns on the motor might be 7_____ fault. One of the following malfunctions is probably holding you up.

1. Your battery is weak or 8_____. When turning on the 9_____ you hear a draggy ruur—instead of a fast-clipped rr-rr—or nothing. Tap 10_____ horn or flick on the headlights. If they 11_____ work either, your battery is flat. What to do: Ask another driver for a push—the engine is 12_____ likely to turn over while your car is moving. 13_____ you're lucky, a neighbour may have a length of cable with crocodile clips. 14_____ can be attached at one end to another car's healthy 15_____ and at the other to your sick one; the transfer of electricity will spark the ignition.

16_____ matter what strategy you use to start the car, next 17_____ you're at a garage, have your 18_____ checked. Just driving the car for a while 19_____ restore a basically healthy battery, but one that's right down may 20_____ to be charged 21_____ the garage, or replaced.

2. Moisture may be keeping your plugs from sparking: the flow of electricity can
22_____ be interrupted by dampness. With 23_____ rag or
paper towel, wipe the moisture 24_____ the wires leading into the
plugs. Unsnap the distributor cap (the round black bit where the wires
25_____ the plugs come out), dry the inside 26_____
replace.

What to do if your horn sticks: You've pressed your horn, and now it won't
27_____ blaring. Try giving the horn button a sharp tap as
28_____ might be stuck at one end. If you 29_____ where
your car's fuse box is, find out 30_____ fuse governs the horn and
remove 31_____. Then proceed cautiously to the nearest garage for
repairs. 32_____ slowly, as the horn fuse probably controls such
essentials as 33_____ petrol gauge, brake lights, windscreen
34_____ or heaters. Or simply open your bonnet, locate the horn-
shaped contraption making 35_____ the racket, and wiggle the wires
leading to it. If 36_____ fails, grab the wires firmly and jerk
37_____ out by the roots. Voltage here is low, so don't worry about
38_____ a shock, and the wires 39_____ easily be mended
which you must do immediately since driving without a working horn is
40_____.

12. The Plasterer's Mate

There's a workman in Britain who earns as much as a company director. He is Max Quarterman, a thirty-three-year-old plasterer's mate.

Max ¹_____ with his wife and three children in an upper middle-class housing estate ²_____ Burnham, not far from London. His neighbours are ³_____ bank managers, airline pilots, business executives and the like, but ⁴_____ seven-bedroom house—worth £50,000—is the ⁵_____ on the estate. The house is crammed with labour-saving ⁶_____ and luxury appliances. Parked outside the house are Max's

£6,000 Lotus sports car and 7_____ wife's £1,000 Morris Mini—both 8_____ new. Indoors is a colour television set worth £400, and the family's 9_____ and joy—a circular bath with gold-plated taps. 10_____ can a plasterer's mate 11_____ all this? The answer says Max, is hard 12_____. He says he soon realized he wasn't particularly clever, and to get the luxuries he wanted 13_____ mean unrelenting physical labour. In partnership with another plasterer, Max 14_____ contract plastering jobs for a local firm. 15_____ owner of that firm, who earns less than Max, describes 16_____ as "human machines", the best and quickest in the trade, 17_____ can do as much in two days as any 18_____ two-man 19_____ can do in two weeks.

How do they manage it? 20_____ by working overtime: they work a 21_____ eight-hour day, five days a week. The secret lies in Max's hod, 22_____ receptacle on a pole in 23_____ he carries the mixed plaster to the site of the 24_____. Max's is a super-hod—it contains seventy-five kilograms of plaster—almost double the usual 25_____; and Max, a strong fellow, runs when he carries it. 26_____ time is thus left to get on with the plastering. In this way they 27_____ shift and lay a seven-and-a-half ton lorry load of plaster in a day. 28_____ man wastes time smoking, and they cut their tea-breaks and midday meal 29_____ to a total of less than an hour a day. As a result Max 30_____ an average of over £200 a week, which is more than four times the average weekly pay in Britain 31_____. In his best week to date he earned £411, and 32_____ he gets as 33_____ as £160 it's a "disaster".

The Quartermans 34_____ have all the material possessions they want. The question is— 35_____ do they go from here?

13. Jenny Lee at University

Jenny Lee, British ex-member of Parliament, describes an experience she had at university. "Most of our lectures at the university were dreary and boring. The lecturer would enter the room and begin to dictate and the students would write down everything that was said. Only once during the four years I attended classes was any attempt made to break away from the mechanical routine.

I was then in my fourth [1]_____ and had enrolled for a post-graduate [2]_____ in education. The class was intended [3]_____ for those of us who expected [4]_____ earn our living as teachers. Professor Godfry Thomson, [5]_____ was the new Chairman of the Education [6]_____, was going to give his introductory [7]_____. We walked into the room, took [8]_____ our pens and note-books and sat [9]_____ as usual to an hour's industrious [10]_____. Straight away the professor told us to [11]_____ away our note-books and pens. [12]_____ would not be needed. He did [13]_____ intend reading aloud to us at dictation pace. It really was not necessary. [14]_____ material was available in book form. This said, smiling in the friendliest way, he [15]_____ for a moment. The poor man [16]_____ have expected some sign of [17]_____. Instead there was mutiny in the [18]_____. Not noisy mutiny. Just sullen, anxious [19]_____. No notes? What did that mean? [20]_____ then could we memorize for examination [21]_____? His next announcement was worse. We [22]_____ to form ourselves into groups, each [23]_____ doing a special piece of reading [24]_____ research and, later in the term, [25]_____ to the general class. That was [26]_____ much. That was taking the ground from [27]_____ our feet altogether. That made the [28]_____ of possible questions when examination time [29]_____ too dangerously varied and unpredictable. A [30]_____ of us were flattered by the [31]_____ professor's expectations and disgusted with the [32]_____ of most of the students who [33]_____ afraid when a university class threatened [34]_____ become anything more serious than memorizing set pieces of dictation. For once I

35_____ myself on the side of authority. 36_____ of course, I had to choose 37_____ occasion when authority was hopelessly out-numbered. 38_____ rebels won. The proposed scheme of work was modified to give a much 39_____ proportion of formal lecturing than had 40_____ originally intended. As far as I 41_____ discover the explanation of this was 42_____ fear. Economic fear. Most of us 43_____ poor students. We could not afford 44_____ take risks. We wanted the old familiar system that enabled us to graduate successfully 45_____ the shortest possible time.

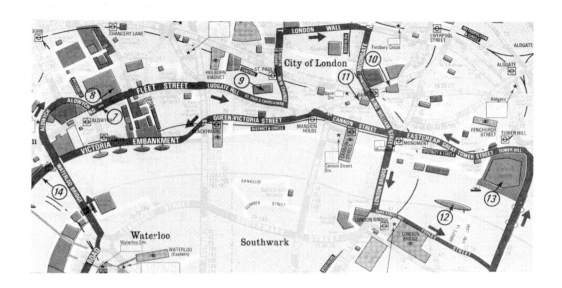

14. London Transport's Round London Sightseeing Tour

There is no guide on this tour, but a leaflet shows the route of the bus on a map of London, and helps to point out places of interest on the way.

You will recognize some of the buildings and London landmarks from the illustrations surrounding the map.

We hope you enjoy your trip. Thank you for joining us.

LONDON—THE LIVING CITY

Over seven million people live or work in London. This tour introduces you to London's famous landmarks and buildings. London is a city of many parts—ceremony, history and tradition are blended to make it among the most interesting and colourful of all great capitals.

Westminster

Royal Westminster [1]_____ the heart of London, for here are the
Houses of Parliament, and [2]_____ country's administration centres
around Whitehall and St. James's. You will be [3]_____ Parliament
Square and the front [4]_____ the Palace of Westminster with its twin
towers of St. Stephens and Victoria. [5]_____ Ben is strictly the name of
the bell which strikes hours in the 320-ft. tower near Westminster Bridge—it has
[6]_____ famous throughout the [7]_____ as a symbol of
London. Look out for Downing Street as you go [8]_____ Whitehall—the
Prime Minister of the day [9]_____ at No. 10. Nearby at Horse Guards,
mounted soldiers on sentry duty [10]_____ be seen. [11]_____
are foot guards outside St. James's Palace and afterwards you
[12]_____ re-visit both places with your camera. Facing the Trafalgar
Square fountains is the National Gallery—and [13]_____ inevitable
London pigeons!

The Royal Parks

On the tour [14]_____ will pass near two Royal Parks. The larger and
[15]_____ famous is Hyde Park. [16]_____ the Marble Arch corner is Speakers' Corner—the world's freest debating society, [17]_____
all may have their say. Kensington Gardens is [18]_____ the western side
of the Park. Green Park, a park [19]_____ any flowers, can be seen on
the left as you [20]_____ down Piccadilly; Buckingham Palace lies at its
south side. The tour [21]_____ not pass the Palace, [22]_____
of Queen Elizabeth, but every visitor should include it in a list of
" [23]_____ " to see. The Guard [24]_____ changed at Buckingham Palace in a colourful ceremony [25]_____ can be seen at least
every other day, without charge. The Royal Parks are [26]_____ to
everyone, and provide a welcome rest for the [27]_____ when weary of
sightseeing.

The City

[28]_____ is the oldest part of London, which was once enclosed
[29]_____ a wall. The Romans knew it, and it is now the
[30]_____ economic, business and insurance centre. The tour
[31]_____ will take you beneath the grey, grim walls of the Tower of

London, 32_____ has become London's 33_____ popular visitor's attraction. The Bank of England, Royal Exchange and Mansion House 34_____ lie close together, so you 35_____ keep a sharp lookout as the bus reaches the Bank intersection. There are still 36_____ churches in the City which 37_____ built by Sir Christopher Wren—his masterpiece is St. Paul's Cathedral, completed 38_____ 1710 and erected on the site of the 39_____ building destroyed in the Great Fire of London, 1666.

London's Riverside

40_____ the bus crosses Lambeth Bridge you 41_____ have a clear view of the Houses of Parliament buildings from 42_____ best aspect—the riverside. You will cross Waterloo Bridge also; once again 43_____ a point of seeing the riverside buildings as 44_____ as the moored ships. You will see the 45_____ again at London Bridge, newest of the Thames 46_____. Old London Bridge was dismantled and re-erected in 47_____ USA. The earliest London Bridge was, for centuries the only bridge 48_____ the lower Thames. The 49_____ bridge used by the tour bus is Tower Bridge—a 50_____ London landmark. It is only rarely now 51_____ the bascules are lifted to permit the passage of large 52_____. The warship on the river is *HMS Belfast.*

15. Postcodes

Customers all over the South-east are starting to find dotty envelopes on their doormats.

The dots—in two lines across the front of the envelope—prove that an increasing amount of mail is now being sorted by machine. Because the ¹_____ cannot read ordinary handwriting, the postcode in each address is converted by a keyboard ²_____ a series of dots.
Electronic eyes in the machines ³_____ read the ⁴_____ and send the letters on towards their destination.
By the end of the year, most of the 30 ⁵_____ letters posted in Britain ⁶_____ day will be handled in automated sorting offices. Already, ⁷_____ of the South Eastern mail is automatically ⁸_____ by machines at Reading, Guildford, Portsmouth, Redhill and Brighton.
Automation is ⁹_____ to the future of the postal service.
¹⁰_____ the collection and ¹¹_____ of letters will always need the human hand, postal services all ¹²_____ the world are particularly prone to the effects of inflation. ¹³_____ sorting machines can help overcome the problem. By sorting letters at very ¹⁴_____ speed—up to 16,000 ¹⁵_____ hour to 150 different destinations—they will help reduce the Post Office's wage bill ¹⁶_____ the problem of finding suffi-cient staff in certain key ¹⁷_____ offices.
Persuading customers to ¹⁸_____ their postcodes is a vital ingredient in the automation of postal sorting. Without a ¹⁹_____ on the envelope only a partial set of dots can be produced, ²⁰_____ the effectiveness of the sorting machines.
²¹_____ encourage customers in the South-east to use ²²_____ postcodes, the Post Office ²³_____ recently sent every household in the region details of their individual postcode. Next month, a free draw with a ²⁴_____ prize of a Mini and over 500 cash ²⁵_____ will take place. Using coloured dots ²⁶_____ of plain ones on machine-sorted envelopes is ²⁷_____ part of the Post Office's vital campaign.

16. The Last Man to Fight Ali?

(This article appeared a few days before Muhammad Ali fought against Larry Holmes in Las Vegas on 2 October 1980. Ali had won the title of boxing heavyweight champion of the world three times and lost it three times. This fight was his attempt to capture it for the fourth time. It was generally thought that this would be Ali's last major fight.)

Larry Holmes, the heavyweight champion of the world, has an identity problem. People in the street call him George (Forman) or Ken (Norton) or even Leon (Spinks). He says that he's fighting for his own identity and for his dignity.

His [1]_____ follows a familiar pattern among American boxers: Southern, black, poor, abandoned [2]_____ his father and raised in the industrial North by his strong, loving [3]_____. The seventh of 12 children, Larry was [4]_____ in Georgia on November 3, 1949, and [5]_____ up in Easton, Pennsylvania. The family was on welfare. Larry [6]_____ shoes, and learned a little street corner poker.

"He always put money [7]_____ in a school savings account. Larry looked after [8]_____" recalls his best friend and distant cousin, Eddie Sutton, [9]_____ now is Larry's driver and assistant. "When [10]_____ came to any sport, from marbles [11]_____ basketball and even drag-car racing he was number one in the valley. He was [12]_____ natural. He even learned to swim [13]_____ himself. I remember, when we were eight or nine, my mother [14]_____ to give him 50 cents a day to teach me to [15]_____ in the Delaware River. Since then, I've always [16]_____ faith in Larry."

As a boy Larry used to take [17]_____ in street fights. At 13 he quit school and [18]_____ 14 he began sparring with professional fighters and signing [19]_____ "the next heavyweight champion of the [20]_____."

He worked hard: car-washing, truck driving, pouring steel in foundries and
21_____ dreamt. "He 22_____ watch Frazier and Norton on
TV and say, 'Give me a couple of years and the chance. 23_____ beat
those guys,' " recalls 24_____ . "But not Ali. Ali was his idol,
25_____ legend."

As an amateur, Holmes lost the big one, the final elimination for the 1972 Olym-
pics. 26_____ 1973, 27_____ 23, he turned professional and
soon cut his teeth as a sparring partner to Frazier and Ali. " 28_____ I
learned from Ali was the left jab 29_____ the face. 'Stick and move,' he
used to 30_____ to me. 'Stick and move because the other guy
31_____ hit what he can't see.' "

32_____ is a good mover. He is a stand up fighter 33_____ he
will work on Ali's vulnerable kidneys and hope, deep down, 34_____
the referee stops the fight 35_____ he hurts the legend of his lifetime.
"The old man ain't gonna 36_____ me," he says; and adds with chill-
ing candour, "The only guy who 37_____ beat me is myself."

17. A Recipe for Steak and Kidney Pie

Give a rich flavour to a steak and kidney pie by stirring into the gravy 2 tablespoons of tomato ketchup and 1 teaspoon of made English mustard before putting the crust on top. Serves 4.

Oven temperature: 350°F, gas mark 4 for 2 hours
425°F, gas mark 7 for 15 minutes
350°F, gas mark 4 for [1]_____ 20 minutes

Total cooking time: approximately 2 [2]_____ 35 minutes

INGREDIENTS

1½ lb. stewing steak
¼ lb. ox kidney
2 tablespoons flour, well seasoned with [3]_____ and pepper
1 large onion, peeled and thinly sliced
2 [4]_____ tomato ketchup
1 teaspoon made English [5]_____
1 (7 oz.) packet puff pastry
egg or milk to glaze

METHOD

1. Wash [6]_____ steak and kidney [7]_____ pat dry on absorbent kitchen paper.

2. Put [8]_____ in a paper [9]_____ plastic bag with the seasoned flour and shake gently to coat.

3. [10]_____ the steak, kidney and onion in a casserole and just cover with water. Put the lid [11]_____ the casserole and [12]_____ in a 350°F, gas mark 4, oven [13]_____ 2 hours, peeping occasionally to see that there is sufficient gravy.

31

4. When the meat [14]_____ cooked, transfer to a pie dish,
[15]_____ enough gravy to half fill the dish. [16]_____ in the
tomato ketchup and mustard.

5. Roll the puff pastry to the thinness of a 10p [17]_____, larger than the
pie dish [18]_____ that a rim can be cut from the outside.
[19]_____ the edge of the pie dish with water and fit the rim
[20]_____ it. Cut side facing down.

6. Damp the pastry edge with [21]_____ and lift on the top of the pie,
[22]_____ stretching the [23]_____. Trim, and flake the edges.

7. Decorate with pastry leaves [24]_____ you like, and brush with beaten
egg or milk.

8. [25]_____ at 425°F, gas mark 7, for 15 minutes, reduce the
[26]_____ to 350°F, gas mark 4, for approximately 20 minutes, or until
the pastry is golden [27]_____ and well puffed-up and cooked.

18. Disneyland

This is an extract from an interview with Ray Bradbury, the science fiction writer, who was talking about life in America in the next decade.

Question: What do you ¹_____ as the country's most pressing problems in the next decade?

Answer: The rebuilding of America. ²_____ runs for President this year ³_____ say, "Okay, we've got a war on our hands, now ⁴_____ go and borrow 40 billion dollars from our weapons for one year, ⁵_____ let's rebuild every major town in the country so that ⁶_____ will have a nice ⁷_____ to live. That's the exciting challenge. It could be great fun, it ⁸_____ really be glorious spending the next 20 or 30 ⁹_____ rebuilding the whole country, ¹⁰_____ that we will all be madly in love with America again. Disneyland and Disney World ¹¹_____ teach us how to rebuild parts of our major cities.

Question: Disneyland?

Answer: ¹²_____ set an ¹³_____ for all of us because he cared about the future. He ¹⁴_____ two ideal communities which serve as examples of ways ¹⁵_____ turning mobs into crowds. Disneyland isn't a fantasy land, ¹⁶_____ a way of architecturally putting together an environment that humanizes us.

Question: For example?

Answer: Disney ¹⁷_____ us seven or ¹⁸_____ alternative ways of travelling in the city: the monorail, the people mover, ¹⁹_____ kinds of trams, trains and escalators, moving sidewalks, small motor cars ²⁰_____ run on fixed courses. Okay, these are toys, ²¹_____ nevertheless, the principle could be applied on a larger scale. ²²_____ musn't look at Disneyland as a frivolous exercise . . . this ²³_____ really cared about us and ²⁴_____ future.

19. Your Daily Horoscope

Aries (March 21–April 19)

Let others set pace at work. An impossible dream may have to be given up. What is still to come will be better than anything you've known in the past. Find a new way of solving a difficult problem.

Taurus (April 20–May 20)

Someone 1_____ brings bad news may be misinformed. Refuse to panic. Eventually, true situation 2_____ revealed. Fine day to show close ties how much they 3_____ to you and gain added goodwill. Be more optimistic 4_____ the future.

Gemini (May 21–June 21)

Be receptive to suggestions of those who 5_____ more experience. Social contacts 6_____ lead to meaningful business associations. Follow instincts for affairs of heart. You have excellent ideas 7_____ should be put into operation quickly for 8_____ results.

Cancer (June 22–July 22)

Postpone costly outings, purchases. Put more thought, time 9_____ work. Contact people who can help you. Find best way to handle tasks 10_____ you have committed 11_____ to and gain the respect of others.

Leo (July 22–August 21)

Learn to be [12]_____ self-reliant and you will save yourself big disappointments. A romantic partner is the [13]_____ person to consult about career change. Study new ideas and [14]_____ the most practical ones. [15]_____ have creative ideas that need expression.

Virgo (August 22–September 22)

Show that you [16]_____ pride in your work. Keep promises you have [17]_____. A time to put more effort in your work. If content to proceed slowly today, [18]_____ goes well. Refuse to get in arguments with [19]_____ who never seems to learn.

Libra (September 23–October 22)

Family members may grumble [20]_____ a change in routine, but eventually they adjust to liking [21]_____. Try to co-operate more with [22]_____ at work and get better results. Avoid one who is [23]_____ time waster.

Scorpio (October 23–November 21)

Start early on business matters so [24]_____ have more time for recreation. Be willing to try new procedures. [25]_____ honest with mate, or spouse about expectations and hopes. Avoid unnecessary spending of [26]_____.

Sagittarius (November 22–December 21)

A fine day to study [27]_____ environment and to make needed improvements. Stay within your budget. Steer clear of situations that could [28]_____ trouble.

Capricorn (December 22–January 19)

Conserve energy, enthusiasm 29_____ important matters. A newcomer displays interest in your ideas and company. Be 30_____ objective in your business dealings and get better results. 31_____ for ways to improve your business status. Show 32_____ that you can be relied upon.

Aquarius (January 21–February 19)

A 33_____ day to finalize business, and financial transactions. Assume a leadership role and others 34_____ fall in with your plans. You may be anxious 35_____ gain a personal aim but 36_____ be forceful with others in trying to do so. Be wise.

Pisces (February 20–March 20)

Go after more of whatever 37_____ is you want, 38_____ be careful in handling varying activities. Think constructively. Do 39_____ tasks early. Creative urges enjoy favorable influence. Conserve money by letting others 40_____ their fair share of expenses in social situations.

20. How to Use Your Washing Machine

Working Instructions and Preparation for Washing

Before using the washing machine it is advisable to run it for a complete cycle with detergent and hot water without linen, with a view to eliminating any possible residue of greasy substances and to ascertaining that it works properly. The superautomatic washing machine [1]_____ stable and noiseless. If during use unusual movements are noticed, make [2]_____ that it is level by altering the adjustable feet. [3]_____ addition, it is a [4]_____ idea to carefully inspect the detergent feeder to [5]_____ certain that it contains no foreign bodies as they [6]_____ damage the washing machine.

Preliminary checks

Before starting the machine ensure that:
—the machine is plugged [7]_____;
—the water supply hose is connected [8]_____ the tap and that this is [9]_____ on;
—the waste water hose is properly hooked over the sink and the outlet [10]_____ blocked.

If the door is not properly [11]_____, the machine will not [12]_____. It should always be remembered that the washing machine is made to wash [13]_____ to eleven pounds of dry linen and before putting the linen inside, [14]_____ (such as coins, keys, [15]_____) must be removed from the pockets and folds of clothes. Take [16]_____ any loose buttons and take out the stiffeners from shirt collars. [17]_____ all zips, and remove anything that can possibly mark or stain the [18]_____. It is better to spread the linen out as [19]_____ as possible in the machine instead [20]_____ crumpling it up.

We wish to emphasize the preliminary operations [21]_____ should be carried out [22]_____ plugging in the machine.

Sorting the clothes

—Whites and strong colours;
—Non-resistant coloureds;
—Delicate 23_____ (silk, nylon, rayon, etc.).

It should be remembered that 24_____ of these groups must be washed separately, as 25_____ all require different water temperatures and different amounts of washing 26_____.

With the superautomatic washing machine in view of 27_____ washing capacity, it is not necessary to prewash shirt 28_____ and cuffs with soap. It is, however, 29_____ to remove all persistent fruit, ink, 30_____ stains, etc., with the usual cleaning methods before putting the linen into the 31_____.

Washing instructions

Washing with the machine is very simple. 32_____ remember these points: sort the clothes, put them into the machine, 33_____ the detergents in the respective feeders and 34_____ the programme and the temperature 35_____ suitable for the type of linen to be washed. Turn 36_____ timer knob until the indicator coincides with the symbol of the chosen 37_____. Finally, pull the 38_____ of the timer outwards.

21. An Interview with Tom Stoppard

Tom Stoppard, who is one of England's leading playwrights, was interviewed on the BBC some time ago.

D.C.: You started work in [1]_____ practical world of words, in journalism. Where did your stagecraft come [2]_____? Did you have a theatrical background in your [3]_____, perhaps—or was it just a personal interest [4]_____ you developed?

T.S.: I had no theatrical background at all. As a [5]_____ of fact, I did come into contact with the theatre in Bristol, [6]_____ the newspaper was. I wrote [7]_____ the theatre, and I met the actors,

8_____ I have a feeling that that's not as relevant as it may seem. I
9_____ that the way to use the theatre is 10_____ something
which one learns. One *senses* how a thing might 11_____ exciting, how
a thing might actually be structured and I don't 12_____ using any experience directly. 13_____ partly common sense and partly just a sort
of intuition.

D.C.: You choose a 14_____ variety of strange characters in your
plays; for 15_____ in *After Magritte,* the central "character"—someone
referred 16_____ by all the people 17_____ the play—is a
one legged footballer hopping through the rain with a tortoise under his arm.
18_____ do you 19_____ your characters from?

T.S.: The specific answer (about *After Magritte*) is that something vaguely similar
happened to an acquaintance of 20_____ who had some peacocks in his
garden. 21_____ day he was shaving and saw that one had escaped. He
22_____ it and caught it, and just as he 23_____ it, the traffic
started going by (24_____ gone about a hundred yards)—and he realized that the people in the cars were looking 25_____ a man in pyjamas
with shaving foam 26_____ his face, carrying a 27_____.
They just saw this man for a second, and for the rest 28_____ their lives
they'd have to work out what 29_____ seen. I don't write about the
man with the peacock—I 30_____ about the people in the cars. It's
31_____ like Rosencrantz and Guildenstern—things just go by
32_____ and they're very difficult to work out.

D.C.: But somewhere within this strangeness, 33_____ logic, isn't
there?

T.S.: That's very important indeed. 34_____ me, the whole exercise is
pointless and empty unless there's a rationale 35_____ it.

22. The Ugly Show

I thought I knew what to expect when I came to cover the beauty queen pageant. I was quite prepared to feel contempt 1————————— the contestants, patronizing towards the audience and 2——————— bored with the whole event. What I was totally unprepared for was to 3——————— pity, sorrow, and revulsion.

4——————— came in wiggling their hips, and teetering on high heels, not 5——————— nervous horses or strutting pigs 6————————— a country fair. This time, we were told, the contestants 7——————— to be tested for intelligence, as well as 8——————— which was only fair, I thought, since even dogs at a dog 9——————— have to turn a few tricks before they 10——————— the blue ribbon.

Being judged—or more often condemned, 11——————— to the audience's comments for their buttocks, breasts and 12———————, the 22 women on the stage were 13——————— what millions of women do daily—competing for 14——————— approval in their enslavement to "beauty" standards that they are conditioned to 15——————— seriously.

Camouflaged with paint, stuffed 16——————— identical skin-tight bathing suits and tiny spindle-heeled 17——————— the beauty queen candidates were difficult 18——————— impossible, to tell apart. 19———————, taller, shorter, over or under the weight prescribed by 20——————— determines what beauty is, doesn't have a chance in this 21———————, where conformity is the key to the crown. 22——————— goes for personality and intelligence 23———————. The rejection of the individual woman in 24——————— game is but a reflection of 25——————— gospel: women must be young and girlish. 26——————— could be more ignored than last year's beauty 27———————? She embodies the 28——————— use, mutilated and discarded.

23. A Whale of a Problem

Do whales sometimes commit suicide? For centuries, men have been wondering about the inexplicable way in which these huge creatures from time to time stubbornly strand themselves on shores throughout the world. The British Museum has details of over 10,000 such incidents during the past 65 years. But whale scientists who study this phenomenon tend [1]_____ reject the suicide theory and split the strandings up [2]_____ single and multiple varieties.

In the first group, where a lone animal beaches [3]_____, careful post-mortem examinations generally show the cause to be disease, injury

4_____ old age. Very often, parasitic worms are 5_____ clogging the lungs or invading the brain. Industrial pollution of 6_____ sea with chemicals 7_____ as mercury can also produce brain damage in areas 8_____ the Baltic Sea.

Multiple strandings, 9_____ groups of perhaps several hundred whales fling 10_____ up on the sand, are more difficult to explain. Gently sloping sandy beaches 11_____ send back confusing sonar echoes, storms at sea, pursuit 12_____ sharks or killer whales, frightening underwater noises (13_____ volcanoes or exploding mines) or following fish shoals 14_____ far inshore, 15_____ all been given as possible reasons. Some scientists have found clusters of parasitic worms 16_____ the ear cavities of multiple 17_____ cases. It's possible 18_____ these parasites interfere with the crucial mechanism of echo-location. Or are the whales instinctively 19_____ the ancient migratory routes of 20_____ land-dwelling ancestors?

The lastest theory suggests that, as whales evolved 21_____ land mammals, they would have passed 22_____ an amphibious half-way stage—neither complete land-livers 23_____ fully aquatic. At that stage of their development, they 24_____ have sought the safety of solid ground when danger threatened. Nowadays perhaps, 25_____ stressed by disease, injury or fear of attack, these fascinating animals subconsciously make 26_____ their ancestral home—a 27_____ which, now that they have lost their limbs over millions of years of evolution, is the 28_____ opposite of welcoming.

24. A Business Letter

British Ballpoint Ltd.,
16 King Charles Street,
London W1.

Thomas Cook & Son,
Berkeley Square,
London W1.

14th September 1981

Dear Sir,

Travel Arrangements: Milan, Italy

Please refer [1]_____ our telephone conversation of last week. I am now
[2]_____ to finalise travel plans for my forthcoming trip to Milan, Italy.

Appointments have been [3]_____ for the 28th September to 1st October
inclusive. I plan, however, to [4]_____ in Milan for personal business on
2nd October. I [5]_____ be grateful if you would make the undermen-
tioned [6]_____ for me.

Travel: Outward—late afternoon or [7]_____ flight on Monday 27th
September, Heathrow to Linate.
Return —morning [8]_____ on Sunday 3rd October, Linate to
[9]_____.

My ticket should be Club Class [10]_____ the possibility of changing my
return reservation, if necessary.

Accommodation: One double room, with bathroom, for six ¹¹_____ from 27th September to 2nd October ¹²_____, in a first-class hotel near La Scala Opera House; upper ¹³_____ limit £50 ¹⁴_____ night inclusive of service. When making the booking, please inform the hotel of the ¹⁵_____ time of my flight so ¹⁶_____ they will hold the room.

Opera tickets: Please instruct your Milan representative to reserve four good seats ¹⁷_____ La Scala ¹⁸_____ the performance on Friday 1st October and to deliver the ¹⁹_____ to my hotel after my arrival.

²⁰_____ inform me as soon as possible of the name and address of the hotel ²¹_____ I shall be accommodated, together ²²_____ the rate agreed.

You should debit the British Ballpoint account in the usual way.

I look ²³_____ to receiving details of the finalised arrangements.

Yours ²⁴_____,

A. V. Johnson

A. V. Johnson

25. When a Volcano Blows its Top

Volcano! At one time people ran from an erupting volcano; now when one erupts, as Mount Etna in Sicily did recently, it's a major tourist attraction. On the islands of Hawaii, people have learnt to live with the constant possibility of a fiery outbreak, and on the main island there are still sudden eruptions.

In 1960, a ¹_____ village in Hawaii was destroyed and 70 buildings were burnt and buried ²_____ the lava. In 1977, there was an ³_____ from another mountain. ⁴_____ time this happens, the lava flows, burning and destroying woods and orchards ⁵_____ leaving a desolate field of cinder and dead trees ⁶_____. You can see such a stretch at the Volcanoes National Park, where not long ⁷_____, a lava flow permanently blocked off 19 km of roadway.

You ⁸_____ still see steam jets forced up from the contact of water ⁹_____ underground lava-heated rocks and, if you're lucky, you ¹⁰_____ even feel a slight underground tremor, for movement is never far ¹¹_____ the surface on the main island. The old dead craters soon fill with ¹²_____ varieties of exotic plants and birds, and even wild pigs ¹³_____ their homes here.

In the park, there is a small pocket of tropical forest ¹⁴_____ the entrance to one of the most interesting manifestations ¹⁵_____ flowing lava—a lava tube.

¹⁶_____ is produced when the surface of a fast-flowing lava stream cools and crusts over, and a tunnel is ¹⁷_____ which can stretch for many kilometres down ¹⁸_____ the ocean. Lava is molten basalt rock which, when cooled, ¹⁹_____ a very good thermal insulator. There are many of these drained "tubes" on Hawaii, and in the park you can walk ²⁰_____ part of one where molten once flowed ²¹_____ 35 km an hour.

The Hawaiian islands were [22]_____ by volcanic action and their mountains are the [23]_____ massive in the world—from seabed to summit they are [24]_____ 11,000 metres in [25]_____. East of the big island, 7,000 metres [26]_____ the surface, another isle is pushing up—but it won't surface for 10,000 years.

26. Positive Discrimination

Will "Positive discrimination" make a reality rather than a formality of equal opportunities for boys and girls, women and men in education and working life? This was one of the crucial questions discussed by twenty-two European ministers of education at the eleventh session of their standing conference in The Hague last June.

Many reports prepared for the conference showed that boys and girls adopt certain sex-role stereotypes even before entering kindergarten. [1]_____ are reinforced all the way up through the [2]_____ system, including university, and show strongly when the young people [3]_____ choosing careers. Consequently it is essential that the pre- and primary schools employ a

48

greater number of 4_____ teachers and the upper end of the educational system more female 5_____ so as to 6_____ "models" for boys and girls. (The aim would be 7_____ only to emancipate girls and women but to change the attitudes of boys and men 8_____.) Educational choices offered to boys and girls 9_____ accordingly be the 10_____. Boys should be trained in domestic responsibilities, not only to be the family bread-winner 11_____ girls should be equipped to earn an independent living, to cope with the technical elements of practical life and to participate 12_____ democratic decision-making and public life. Special attention should be 13_____ to the nature 14_____ extent of sex-role stereotyping in school teaching materials, time-tabling and educational and 15_____ guidance. This calls for initial and in-service training courses to 16_____ educators to be 17_____ of and to be able to counteract prevalent 18_____.

27. Appliance Guarantee

Any part which becomes defective under normal and proper use, during a period of 1 year from date of installation, will be repaired or replaced f.o.b. factory, provided that the appliance is installed by an authorized White-Westinghouse International Distributor or his Service Organization, in accordance with the instructions provided at the time of purchase, and subject to the "Exceptions" listed below.

EXCEPTIONS

1. This guarantee shall be null [1]_____ void if the serial number attached [2]_____ this appliance is removed or otherwise illegible.
2. [3]_____ appliance is designed for private family use and the guarantee does not [4]_____ if this appliance is used for any other purpose.
3. This [5]_____ does not apply to the exterior cabinet, its finish [6]_____ any part of the cabinet whatsoever.
4. Costs due [7]_____ accidents, misuse, abuse, or alterations to the appliance are [8]_____ covered by this guarantee and are the responsibility of [9]_____ owner.
   Examples of this, but without limitations [10]_____:
   a. Foreign objects in the appliance.
   b. Improper load, improper use of bleaches [11]_____ detergents.
   c. Appliance connected to improper voltages or cycles, defective [12]_____ inadequate wiring, defective or open fuses or circuit breakers.
   d. Inadequate or improper plumbing, water, or gas [13]_____.
5. White Westinghouse [14]_____ not be responsible for any labor costs including, but not limited [15]_____, the labor costs to analyze the condition of the [16]_____, or the labor costs incurred in the replacement of any part.
   The [17]_____ or replacement of such inoperative parts [18]_____ constitute complete fulfilment of all the obligations of White-Westinghouse [19]_____ respect to this appliance. Labor,

transportation, local duties and taxes required ²⁰_____ the responsibility of the owner. White-Westinghouse shall not ²¹_____
responsible in any event for consequential damages.
White-Westinghouse authorizes no ²²_____ to change or add to any
of White-Westinghouse's obligations ²³_____ this warranty. Any
parts obtained from any source other ²⁴_____ White-Westinghouse
distributors, dealers or service companies are not ²⁵_____ by
²⁶_____ warranty.

EXCEPT AS SET FORTH HEREIN WHITE-WESTINGHOUSE INTER-
NATIONAL COMPANY MAKES ²⁷_____ OTHER
WARRANTY OR GUARANTEE EXPRESSED, IMPLIED OR
STATUTORY, INCLUDING ²⁸_____ IMPLIED
WARRANTY OF MERCHANTABILITY OR FITNESS FOR
²⁹_____ PARTICULAR PURPOSE.

28. Child Custody

A century ago, fathers who fought in court for custody of their children usually won, simply because they were the breadwinners. Early in this century, women began persuading judges that [1]_____ were better suited to child-rearing, and courts [2]_____ awarding them custody and child-support payments. As one judge [3]_____ in 1921, for a youngster of "tender years [4]_____ can be an adequate substitute [5]_____ mother love."

Most judges today still hold to this standard. Each [6]_____ courts determine the fate of some 100,000 children of divorce and, in [7]_____ out of ten cases, the mother gets [8]_____. Another 900,000 children a year are similarly dispersed out of court. [9]_____ the belief is growing that mothers aren't necessarily the [10]_____ parents after a divorce. Neither [11]_____ fathers.

A new arrangement has [12]_____ evolving, mostly in private divorce settlements, known as joint custody. The parents agree to [13]_____ equally in important decisions regarding their [14]_____, and to share fairly, though not always equally, in their physical care. A [15]_____ state legislatures have authorized joint custody if judges find it in a [16]_____ best interest. In other states, like New York, judges have [17]_____ joint custody awards without requiring special [18]_____.

29. Ronald Reagan Accepts Nomination

An extract from a speech made by Ronald Reagan at the Republican National Convention in Detroit in July 1980, after being voted the official Republican candidate

"I ask you to trust that American spirit which knows no ethnic, religious, social, political, regional, or economic boundaries; the spirit that burned with zeal in the hearts of millions of immigrants from every corner of the Earth who came here in search of freedom.

"Some say that spirit no longer exists. [1]_____ I have seen it—I have felt [2]_____—all across the land; in the big cities, the [3]_____ towns, and in rural America. The American spirit is still [4]_____, ready to blaze into life if you and I are [5]_____ to do what has to be [6]_____; the practical, down-to-earth things that will stimulate our economy, [7]_____ productivity, and put America back to work.

"The time is now [8]_____ limit federal spending; to insist [9]_____ a stable monetary reform, and to free [10]_____ from imported oil.

"The time is now to resolve [11]_____ the basis of a firm and principled foreign [12]_____ is one that takes the world as it [13]_____ and seeks to change it by leadership and example; [14]_____ by lecture and harangue.

"The time is now to say that [15]_____ we shall seek new friendships and expand and improve others, we shall not do so by [16]_____ our word or casting aside old [17]_____ and allies.

"And the time is now to redeem promises once [18]_____ to the American people by another candidate, in another [19]_____ and another place.

"[20]_____ three long years I have been going up and [21]_____ this country preaching that government—federal state, and local—costs too much. I [22]_____ not stop that preaching. As an immediate program of action, [23]_____ must abolish useless offices. We [24]_____

53

eliminate unnecessary functions of government. . . .

"We must consolidate subdivisions of government 25_____, like the private citizen, give up luxuries which we can no 26_____ afford.

"I propose to you, my 27_____, and through you that government of all kinds, big and 28_____ be made solvent and that the example be 29_____ by the President of the United States and his cabinet.''

"So 30_____ Franklin Delano Roosevelt in his acceptance 31_____ to the Democratic National Convention in July, 1932.

"The 32_____ is now, my fellow 33_____, to recapture our destiny, to take it into our own hands. But, to do this will 34_____ many of us, working 35_____. I ask you tonight to volunteer your help in this cause 36_____ we can carry our message throughout the land.

"Yes, 37_____ now the time that we, the people, carried out 38_____ unkept promises? Let us pledge to each 39_____ and all America on this July day 48 years 40_____, we intend to do just that.''

30. The New Zealand Home in the 80's

The home is the focus of the nation's life. Other countries go out for entertainment—Englishmen to sit in pubs, Ulstermen to murder each other in the
streets. Kiwi homes are so much bigger, 1_____ and more beautiful,
veritable people's palaces, that the occupants don't want 2_____ leave.
The homes are also so expensive they can't afford 3_____. The home is
the venue for 4_____ most popular forms of entertainment: television,
gardening, and peering 5_____ of the window. It's 6_____ a
hobby you inhabit, and so exhausting that no New Zealander 7_____
calls his house "Mon Repos".

Americans flee the noisy 8_____ to the quiet of suburbia. If you want
weekend peace you must 9_____ away from town. The suburbs
10_____ a cacophony of power drills, motor mowers, hammers, carpet

and child beating [11]_____ revving cars, all punctuated by the screams of amateur roof menders falling [12]_____ their deaths. A New Zealand house begins life [13]_____ a 1,000-square [14]_____ wood or brick box, sitting in a sea of mud and rubble rather like Passchendaele. Within [15]_____ the garden is a condensed and improved version [16]_____ Versailles, likely to turn Capability Brown green with [17]_____. Hand-manicured lawns get more care and attention than the owner's [18]_____. Vegetable gardens carry a crop large [19]_____ to feed the entire Vietcong for decades.

The house's turn comes next. First a decoration, [20]_____ an extension and enlargement, then an [21]_____ and enlargement to the extension and [22]_____. Once the major work is done, maintenance, redecoration and the addition of [23]_____ occasional bedroom or ballroom keeps things going until [24]_____ time to move on and begin over again. The [25]_____ home is his castle. It's the New [26]_____ mistress.